Congressional Research Service
Informing the legislative debate since 1914

Nigeria: Current Issues and U.S. Policy

Lauren Ploch
Specialist in African Affairs

November 15, 2013

Congressional Research Service

7-5700

www.crs.gov

RL33964

Summary

The U.S. government considers its relationship with Nigeria, Africa's largest producer of oil and its second largest economy, to be among the most important on the continent. Nigeria is Africa's most populous country, with more than 170 million people, roughly divided between Muslims and Christians. U.S. diplomatic relations with Nigeria, which is regularly among the top suppliers of U.S. oil imports, have improved since the country made the transition from military to civilian rule in 1999, and Nigeria is a major recipient of U.S. foreign aid. The country is an influential actor in African politics, having mediated disputes in several African countries and ranking among the top five troop contributors to U.N. peacekeeping missions.

Nigeria is a country of significant promise, but it also faces serious social, economic, and security challenges that have the potential to threaten both state and regional stability, and to affect global oil prices. The country has faced intermittent political turmoil and economic crises since independence. Political life has been scarred by conflict along ethnic, geographic, and religious lines, and corruption and misrule have undermined the state's authority and legitimacy. Despite extensive oil and natural gas resources, Nigeria's human development indicators are among the world's lowest, and a majority of the population faces extreme poverty. Years of social unrest, criminality, and corruption in the oil-producing Niger Delta have hindered oil production, delayed the southern region's economic development, and contributed to piracy in the Gulf of Guinea. Perceived neglect and economic marginalization also fuel resentment in the predominately Muslim north. Thousands have been killed in periodic ethno-religious clashes in the past decade.

The attempted terrorist attack on an American airliner by a Nigerian in 2009 and the rise of a militant Islamist group, Boko Haram, have heightened concerns about extremist recruitment in Nigeria, which has one of the world's largest Muslim populations. Boko Haram has increasingly targeted churches, among other state and civilian targets, sometimes triggering retaliatory violence and threatening to inflame religious tensions. While the group remains primarily focused on a domestic agenda, some of its members appear to have expanded ties with other violent Islamist groups, including Al Qaeda in the Islamic Maghreb (AQIM). A Boko Haram splinter group, Ansaru, appears intent on kidnapping foreigners. The State Department designated both Boko Haram and Ansaru as Foreign Terrorist Organizations (FTOs) in November 2013.

Nigeria's last elections, in 2011, were viewed by many as a key test of the government's commitment to democracy. The U.S. government had deemed previous elections to be deeply flawed. Election observers described the 2011 polls as a significant improvement over previous efforts, but not without problems. Post-election protests and violence across the north highlighted communal tensions, grievances, and mistrust of the government in that region. President Goodluck Jonathan, a southerner, was reelected and faces multiple, and sometimes competing, pressures to implement reforms to address Nigeria's security and development challenges.

The Obama Administration has been supportive of Nigerian reform initiatives, including anti-corruption efforts, economic and electoral reforms, energy sector privatization, and programs to promote peace and development in the Niger Delta. In 2010, the Administration established the U.S.-Nigeria Binational Commission, a strategic dialogue to address issues of mutual concern. Congress regularly monitors Nigerian political developments, and some Members have expressed concern with corruption, human rights abuses, environmental damage from oil drilling, and the threat of violent extremism in Nigeria. Congress oversees an estimated $700 million in U.S. foreign aid programs in Nigeria—one of the largest U.S. bilateral assistance packages in Africa.

Contents

Figures

Tables

Contacts

Overview

Nigeria is considered a key power on the African continent, not only because of its size, but because of its political and economic role in the region. One in five people in Sub-Saharan Africa call Nigeria home. The country's commercial center, Lagos, is among the world's largest cities. Nigeria's economy appears set to overtake South Africa's as Sub-Saharan Africa's largest in 2014, and it is one of the world's major sources of high-quality crude oil. Nigerian leaders have mediated conflicts throughout Africa, and Nigerian troops have played a key role in peace and stability operations on the continent. The country ranks among the top five troop contributors to United Nations peacekeeping missions. Few countries in Africa have the capacity to make a more decisive impact on the region.

Despite its oil wealth, however, Nigeria remains highly underdeveloped. Poor governance and corruption have limited infrastructure development and social service delivery, slowing economic growth and keeping much of the country mired in poverty. Nigeria is also home to the world's second-largest HIV/AIDS-infected population and has Africa's highest tuberculosis burden.

The country is home to more than 250 ethnic groups, but the northern Hausa and Fulani, the southwestern Yoruba, and the southeastern Ibo have traditionally been the most politically active and dominant. Roughly half the population, primarily those residing in the north, are Muslim. Southern Nigeria is predominantly Christian.

Ethnic and religious strife have been common in Nigeria. Divisions among ethnic groups, between north and south, and between Christians and Muslims often stem from issues relating to access to land, jobs, and socioeconomic development, and are sometimes fueled by politicians. By some estimates, 15,000 Nigerians have died in localized clashes driven by such tensions in the last decade, including more than 800 people killed in 2011 in post-election clashes. That violence highlighted growing dissatisfaction with the government in Nigeria's northern states.

An increasingly active violent Islamist group, Boko Haram, has contributed to deteriorating security conditions in the north and seeks to capitalize on local frustrations and discredit the government. In November 2013, the U.S. State Department formally designated Boko Haram and a splinter group, Ansaru, as Foreign Terrorist Organizations (FTOs). U.S. policymakers appear particularly concerned with Boko Haram's reported ties with transnational terrorist groups and with the threat these groups may pose to U.S. and international targets, either in the region or overseas. Further, Boko Haram's attacks against churches have the potential to inflame sectarian tensions across Nigeria and, potentially, beyond.

In the southern Niger Delta region, local grievances related to oil production in the area have fueled simmering conflict and criminality for over a decade. The government's efforts to negotiate with local militants, including through an amnesty program, have quieted the restive region, but the peace is fragile and violent criminality continues. Some militants continue to be involved in various local and transnational criminal activity, including maritime piracy and drug and weapons trafficking networks. These networks often overlap with oil theft networks, which contribute to the rising trend of piracy off the coast of Nigeria and the wider Gulf of Guinea, now one of the most dangerous bodies of water in the world.

Figure 1. Nigeria at a Glance

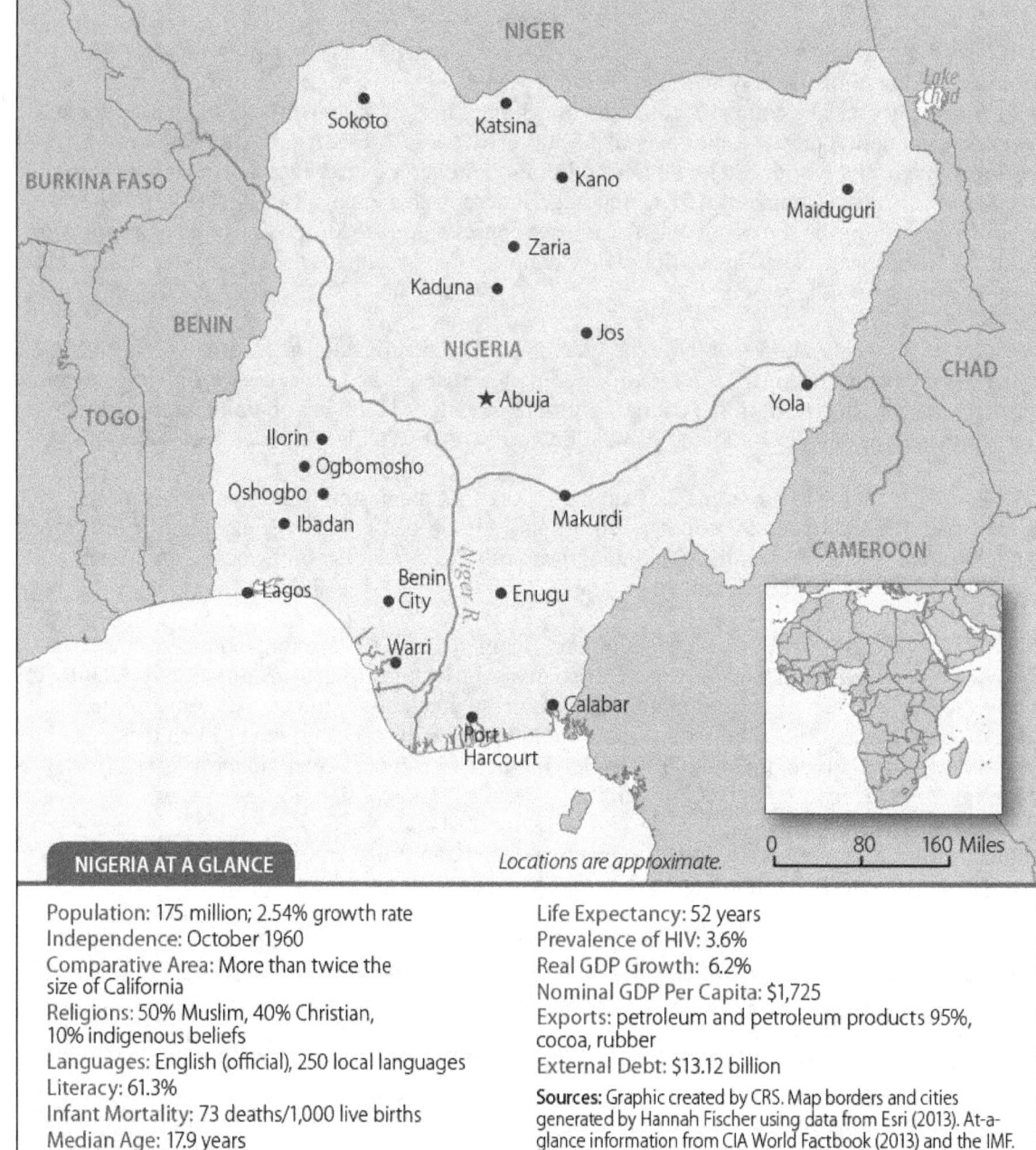

NIGERIA AT A GLANCE — *Locations are approximate.*

Population: 175 million; 2.54% growth rate	Life Expectancy: 52 years
Independence: October 1960	Prevalence of HIV: 3.6%
Comparative Area: More than twice the size of California	Real GDP Growth: 6.2%
	Nominal GDP Per Capita: $1,725
Religions: 50% Muslim, 40% Christian, 10% indigenous beliefs	Exports: petroleum and petroleum products 95%, cocoa, rubber
Languages: English (official), 250 local languages	External Debt: $13.12 billion
Literacy: 61.3%	**Sources:** Graphic created by CRS. Map borders and cities generated by Hannah Fischer using data from Esri (2013). At-a-glance information from CIA World Factbook (2013) and the IMF.
Infant Mortality: 73 deaths/1,000 live births	
Median Age: 17.9 years	

Political Context

Nigeria, which gained its independence from Britain in 1960, is a federal republic with 36 states; its political structure is similar to that of the United States. It has a bicameral legislature with a 109-member Senate and a 360-member House of Representatives. Nigeria's president, legislators, and governors are directly elected on four-year terms. The country was ruled by the military for much of the four decades after independence before making the transition to civilian rule in 1999. Elections held in the decade after the transition were deemed by Nigerians and the international community to be flawed, with each poll progressively worse than the last. The most recent elections, in April 2011, showed serious improvements, but also highlighted outstanding issues.

The contest for power between north and south that has broadly defined much of Nigeria's modern political history can be traced, in part, to administrative divisions instituted during Britain's colonial administration.[1] Northern military leaders dominated the political scene from independence until the transition to democracy just over a decade ago. Since the election of President Olusegun Obasanjo in 1999, there has been a de-facto power sharing arrangement, often referred to as "zoning," between the country's geopolitical zones, through which the presidency was expected to rotate among regions. The death of President Obasanjo's successor, President Umaru Yar'Adua, in office in 2010,[2] and the subsequent ascension of his vice president, Goodluck Jonathan, a former governor from the southern Niger Delta, to the presidency for the remainder of Yar'Adua's first term, raises questions about the future of the zoning arrangement, which is discussed below. President Jonathan's decision to vie for the presidency in 2011, and his electoral victory, further complicates the regional rotation formula.

Elections: The 2011 Polls and a Look Ahead to 2015

Nigeria's ability to weather the potential political crisis of President Yar'Adua's hospitalization and death in office, and to manage the transition without the military playing an apparent role, was viewed by many as positive sign of its democratic progress. After assuming office, President Jonathan continued electoral reforms begun under his predecessor, including efforts to increase the autonomy of the election commission, whose credibility had been badly damaged by previous polls. Jonathan won praise for replacing the commission's chairman with a respected academic and civil society activist, Attahiru Jega, enhancing public confidence prior to the 2011 elections.[3]

With over 73 million registered voters, almost 120,000 polling stations, and more than 50 political parties, however, the challenges facing the election commission in 2011 were daunting. Observers noted positive developments prior to the elections, including efforts to compile a more credible voter register, but also raised concerns about electoral preparedness and areas deemed problematic in previous polls, including ballot secrecy, intimidation, and transparency in the counting of ballots and tabulation of results. Last-minute court rulings on the parties' candidate lists slowed the delivery of voting materials, which in turn delayed the election period by a week.

Given Nigeria's unwritten "zoning" arrangement, there was considerable debate on whether Jonathan's decision to stand for the presidency would lead the ruling party to split prior to the 2011 elections. Many northerners argued that since Obasanjo, who is from the southwest, had served two terms and Yar'Adua, who was from the north, had served only one term, a northern

---

[1] Britain administered the north and south separately from the late 19th century until 1947, when it introduced a federal system that divided the country into three regions: Northern, Eastern, and Western. Today, Nigeria is comprised of six geopolitical zones: north-west, north-east, north-central, south-west, south-east, and south-south (the Niger Delta).

[2] Many speculate that Yar'Adua suffered from a chronic kidney condition. His hospitalization abroad in late 2009 and prolonged absence threatened to spark a political crisis in early 2010, amid rumors of his death, allegations that his wife and close advisors were making decisions for him, and legal challenges related to his failure to transfer power during his convalescence. After several months of uncertainty, the National Assembly recognized Jonathan as the acting head of state in February 2010, allowing him to conduct critical government business. In May 2010, the government announced President Yar'Adua's death at age 58, and Jonathan was sworn in as the new president.

[3] International Crisis Group (ICG), "Nigeria's Elections: Reversing the Degeneration?" February 24, 2011.

candidate should hold the office for another term. Jonathan, who notably is from a minority southeastern ethnic group (the Ijaw), ultimately gained the support of key People's Democratic Party (PDP) leaders, including a majority of the northern governors, for his candidacy, and he won the PDP primary by a wide margin. The leading opposition parties, presumably following zoning, chose northern presidential candidates—former military leader Muhammadu Buhari, who had run in 2003 and 2007, for the Congress for Progressive Change (CPC) and Nuhu Ribadu, the former head of Nigeria's anti-corruption authority, for the Action Congress of Nigeria (ACN).

Figure 2. Results of the 2011 Presidential Election

Source: BBC, adapted by CRS.

The PDP remained the dominant party in the elections, retaining the presidency and a majority in the House of Representatives and most state legislatures. Voters expressed their dissatisfaction, however, by voting out two-thirds of the incumbents in the House and Senate. Opposition candidates made significant gains in the southwest and the north.[4] President Jonathan won 59.6% of the vote, gaining a majority in 23 states and enough support nationwide to avoid a run-off.

---

[4] The ACN dominated state elections in the southwest, where the PDP lost all governors' races and kept a majority in only one state assembly. Nationally, out of 36 states, opposition parties now have 13 governors and 10 state assemblies.

Buhari followed with 32.3% of the votes, leading in one-third of the states (see **Figure 2**). Given Buhari's electoral success in the north, Jonathan's victory was seen by some northern youth as evidence that the results had been rigged, triggering protests that, in some areas, turned deadly.

U.S. government views on the elections were broadly positive, despite the violence. Secretary of State Hillary Clinton declared, "This historic event marks a dramatic shift from decades of failed elections," but stated that "while this election was a success for the people of Nigeria, it was far from perfect."[5] Another senior official noted "technical imperfections," but argued that "this reverses a downward democratic trajectory and provides the country a solid foundation for strengthening its electoral procedures and democratic institutions." President Obama remarked that "the success of the elections was a testament to Nigerian voters who ... were determined that these elections mark a new chapter in Nigerian history."

Election observers generally noted significant improvements in the legislative and presidential polls, calling them a key step forward, but most stopped short of terming the elections "free and fair."[6] Some raised concerns with presidential results from certain states in the Niger Delta (President Jonathan's home region) and the southeast, where turnout appeared to be near 100% amid reports of intimidation, harassment, and violence. Nationally, under-age voting was a common concern of observers, and overcrowding at polling stations and complicated vote collation procedures vulnerable to error or malfeasance remained a problem. Some of the state elections were deemed to be less credible by observers. Various parties filed legal suits challenging the results of the 2011 elections, with varying success. Nigeria's Supreme Court upheld a verdict rejecting the CPC's challenge to President Jonathan's win in December 2011.

Nigeria's next elections are scheduled for 2015, and President Jonathan is expected to run for a second term, although he has yet to formally announce his intentions.[7] The four largest opposition parties have formed a new coalition, the All Progressive Congress (APC), that could pose a serious challenge to the ruling party, should it be able to maintain cohesion through the elections and unite behind a single presidential candidate. The ruling PDP is also struggling with increasing internal divisions as the 2015 elections approach, following the emergence of a splinter faction, known as "the new PDP," in 2013. The splinter group includes seven state governors (all but one from the north) and a sizeable number of members of both the House and the Senate. The group reflects internal power struggles leading up to the party's primaries, which are expected in 2014, and represents opposition, largely but not exclusively from northern party members, to Jonathan's re-election bid. Like the PDP, the APC may struggle to determine how to address the zoning issue, as its most prominent leaders, including Buhari and Lagos Governor Babatunde Fashola, represent different regions of the country. There is speculation that some members of "the new PDP" could join the APC as the elections approach. Various attempts by senior PDP leaders to mend the party's internal rifts have, been unsuccessful, to date, and the continued political tensions could prove an increasing distraction for President Jonathan from other governance and security priorities as 2015 nears. In the interim, donors, including the United States, and advocacy

---

[5] Official comments cited herein include Secretary of State Hillary Clinton, *Press Release: Election in Nigeria*, April 19, 2011; Special Briefing by Assistant Secretary Johnnie Carson, "The Recent Elections in Nigeria," April 28, 2011; and the White House, *Statement by President Obama on Elections in Nigeria*, May 4, 2011.

[6] The author served as an election observer in Lagos for the parliamentary elections and Sokoto for the presidential poll. See the official observer reports of the National Democratic Institute (www.ndi.org); the European Union (eeas.europa.eu/eueom/missions/2011/nigeria); Project 2011 Swift Count (http://www.pscnigeria.org); and the Transition Monitoring Group (http://www.tmgelection2011.org).

[7] A Nigerian court ruled in March 2013 that Jonathan is serving his first term and is thus eligible to run in 2015.

---

groups have stressed the need for the Jonathan government to continue to improve electoral procedures and to prosecute those responsible for electoral fraud during the 2011 elections.[8]

Election-Related Violence in 2011

Despite generally positive reviews of the 2011 elections, the level of election-related violence was higher than in previous years. Deadly clashes that followed the presidential vote highlighted communal tensions, disaffection, and mistrust of the state in the under-developed north—issues that the federal government may have considered a secondary priority in the past decade as it grappled with militant activity in the oil-producing Niger Delta.

Violence prior to the 2011 elections included clashes between party supporters and several assassinations, and some politicians deployed "thugs" to intimidate opponents and voters. Security concerns were further heightened by a spate of bombings during political rallies, primarily in the Delta, that were linked to local politics. There were at least six bombings in the northeast state of Borno, where Boko Haram has been most active. Boko Haram was linked to the assassination of that state's leading gubernatorial candidate, as well as to the bombing of a state election commission headquarters not far from the national capital, Abuja. The government increased security during the polls, and election observer comments were generally positive regarding security forces' behavior during the elections.

The worst violence in 2011 came almost immediately after the presidential poll, with supporters of Muhammadu Buhari leading protests in the northern states, alleging that the PDP had rigged the vote. The protests devolved into violent riots and, in some areas, killings, largely along religious and ethnic lines. In some parts of the north, the clashes lasted for several days until soldiers were deployed to enforce stability. At least 800 people were killed in a three-day period, according Human Rights Watch, and as many as 65,000 displaced. An independent panel, tasked with conducting an official government inquiry into the violence and led by a prominent Islamic scholar, faulted successive administrations for failing to act on the recommendations of previous inquiries into communal and political violence. The panel viewed the zoning arrangement as having politicized ethno-religious tensions and also suggested that statements made by politicians such as Buhari for supporters to "guard their votes" may have fueled popular frustrations and, possibly inadvertently, sparked acts of violence.

Development Challenges and Reform Initiatives

Despite its oil wealth and large economy, Nigeria's population is among Africa's poorest, and the distribution of wealth is highly unequal. The average life expectancy for Nigerians is 52 years, and the percentage of the population living in absolute poverty (less than $1.25 a day) has grown in the past decade. Nigeria has the world's second-largest HIV/AIDS population, after South Africa. Access to clean water remains a major problem—almost half the population has no access to improved sources of water, less than one-fifth of households have piped water, and some 30% lack access to adequate sanitation. Diarrhea is the second-leading cause of death among children, and Nigeria ranks second only to India in the number of diarrhea-related child deaths globally.

Decades of economic mismanagement, instability, and corruption have hindered investment in Nigeria's education and social services systems and stymied industrial growth. U.S. officials suggest that "good governance, healthy political competition, and equitable economic growth would go a long way" to addressing the country's development challenges.[9] The economy depends heavily on the oil and gas sector, which accounts for the majority of government revenues and export earnings. This makes the country particularly vulnerable to swings in global oil prices, and to conflict and criminality in the Niger Delta. Nigeria has averaged real annual GDP growth of almost 7% in the past six years, and is forecast to average above 7% in the

---

[8] See, e.g., ICG, *Lessons From Nigeria's 2011 Elections*, Africa Briefing No. 81, September 15, 2011.

[9] Testimony of Assistant Secretary of State for African Affairs Linda Thomas-Greenfield, in U.S. Congress, House Subcommittee on Africa, Global Health, and Human Rights, *Countering the Threat Posed by Boko Haram*, 113th Cong., November 13, 2013.

coming years. Economists suggest that the economy, which is expected to overtake South Africa's in 2014 as the continent's largest, is nevertheless underperforming, held back by poor infrastructure and electricity shortages. The manufacturing and telecommunications sectors are growing, though, and the banking sector has been a strong performer. Agricultural production contributes over one-third of Gross Domestic Product (GDP) and employs more than two-thirds of the workforce. Nigeria is the largest recipient of foreign direct investment (FDI) in Africa,[10] and it aims to be among the world's top 20 economies by 2020, although insecurity in the north, persistent corruption, and a challenging business environment threaten long-term growth.

When Goodluck Jonathan assumed power in early 2010 from the ailing President Yar'Adua, he vowed to continue his predecessor's various reform initiatives and made public commitments to "restoring Nigeria's image" abroad, both by continuing to act as a key partner in regional peace and counterterrorism efforts, and by ending the "culture of impunity" in Nigeria in terms of corruption and human rights concerns. Those initiatives are discussed briefly below.

Efforts to Combat Corruption

Corruption in Nigeria is "massive, widespread, and pervasive," according to the U.S. State Department, and by many accounts, the country's development will be hampered until it can address the perception of impunity for corruption and fraud.[11] Human Rights Watch suggests that Nigeria's political system rewards rather than punishes corruption, which has been fueled by oil revenues for decades.[12]

According to the Economic and Financial Crimes Commission (EFCC), a Nigerian law enforcement agency created in 2003 to combat corruption and fraud, billions of dollars have been expropriated by political and military leaders since oil sales began in the 1970s.[13] The country's central bank governor has estimated that Nigeria may lose more than 10% of its annual GDP through fraud, and a task force appointed by President Jonathan found in late 2012 than billions of dollars have been lost since 2002 through oil theft and the mispricing of gas exports.[14] Several international firms have been implicated in Nigerian bribery scandals.[15] Nigeria is known globally for cyber crimes, including "419 scams," so-named for the article in the country's penal code that outlaws fraudulent e-mails.

Successive presidents have taken a public stance against corruption, but some observers suggest that they have also used corruption charges to sideline critics and political opponents. President

---

[10] U.N. Conference on Trade and Development (UNCTAD), *World Investment Report 2012*, May 7, 2012.

[11] State Department, "Nigeria," *Country Report on Human Rights Practices 2012*, April 2013.

[12] HRW, *Corruption on Trial? The Record of Nigeria's Economic and Financial Crimes Commission,* August 2011.

[13] Former dictator Sani Abacha reportedly stole more than $3.5 billion during his five years as head of state (1993-1998). Some stolen funds have been repatriated, but other Abacha assets remain frozen abroad.

[14] "Nigeria: Dazzling Statistics," *Africa Confidential*, Vol. 53 No. 14, July 6, 2012; and "The $100 Billion Bash," *Africa Confidential*, November2, 2012.

[15] Among the firms implicated have been German telecom giant Siemens and the U.S. firm Halliburton and its subsidiary Kellogg, Brown, and Root, Inc. (KBR). Halliburton and KBR have paid several hundred million dollars in U.S. and Nigerian fines, and in 2012 the former head of KBR was sentenced to prison in the United States, for bribing Nigerian officials in exchange for contracts worth over $6 billion. The EFCC brought charges against former U.S. Vice President Dick Cheney in 2010 based on his tenure as Halliburton's chief executive; the charges were dropped after the company agreed to a $250 million fine.

Yar'Adua campaigned on an anti-corruption agenda; in 1999 he was the first governor to publicly declare his assets. Upon assuming the presidency, he distanced himself from his predecessor, dismissing many of Obasanjo's political appointees and security chiefs and overturning several of the privatization agreements approved by the former president, amid charges of corruption associated with the sales. Yar'Adua also proposed, unsuccessfully, that the constitution be amended to remove an immunity clause that prevents the president, vice president, governors, and deputy governors from being prosecuted for corruption while in office.

Nevertheless, critics contend that executive interference with the EFCC continued during Yar'Adua's tenure, undermining the entity's investigations and derailing prosecutions. Donors were highly critical of the transfer and eventual dismissal of the EFCC's first chairman, Nuhu Ribadu, in late 2007.[16] President Jonathan fired Ribadu's successor, who was implicated in corrupt practices, in late 2011, replacing her with Ribadu's former deputy, Ibrahim Lamorde. Advocacy groups welcomed Lamorde's appointment, but have called on Jonathan to increase the EFCC's independence, suggesting that the chairman "remains deeply vulnerable to the whims of the president and lacks security of tenure."[17] The U.S. government also signaled its support for Lamorde, and has welcomed other anti-corruption initiatives by the Jonathan government, including the passage of a Freedom of Information law in 2011, a parliamentary inquiry into fraud associated with the country's fuel subsidy program (see below), and the appointment of Ribadu to lead an independent audit of the oil and gas sector. The Jonathan Administration has also pledged to expand budget transparency by requiring legislators and other senior officials to publicly declare their assets, although the extent of the president's own assets remains unknown.[18]

Petroleum and Power Sector Reforms

President Jonathan has also pledged to reform the oil and gas industry, which has been plagued by corruption for decades. Nigeria's first female oil minister, Diezani Allison-Madueke, a former Royal Dutch Shell executive, is leading the government's efforts to pass and implement the ambitious Petroleum Industry Bill (PIB), which is aimed at increasing transparency in the industry, attracting investors, and creating jobs. Progress on the legislation, however, has been halting. The PIB would restructure the Nigerian National Petroleum Corporation (NNPC), the parastatal that oversees regulation of the industry and has been criticized for its lack of transparency. The bill has drawn debate, in part, over a proposed community development fund for the Delta that would be financed from national oil profits.

Nigeria was designated compliant with the Extractive Industries Transparency Initiative (EITI), a global standard for transparency in the oil, gas, and mining sectors, in 2011, indicating that Nigeria had fulfilled the minimum criterion of annually declaring its extractive sector revenues. This does not necessarily suggest that Nigeria has taken aggressive steps to curb corruption in the sector. The United States and other donors welcomed Jonathan's appointment in 2012 of former EFCC Chairman Nuhu Ribadu to lead a new task force to audit oil revenues. Ribadu's task force

---

[16] There was speculation that Ribadu's removal from office was linked to his effort to prosecute former Delta State Governor James Ibori, one of Yar'Adua's primary financial contributors, who may have embezzled over $200 million while in office. First arrested in 2007 and later acquitted, Ibori was indicted again in 2010 but eluded capture and fled to Dubai, where he was arrested by Interpol. He was extradited in 2011 to the United Kingdom, where he owned property and kept some of his assets; he was convicted in 2012 on money laundering and fraud charges.

[17] HRW, *Corruption on Trial? The Record of Nigeria's Economic and Financial Crimes Commission,* August 2011.

[18] U.S.-Nigeria Binational Commission, *Joint Communique,* June 2012.

issued a report in late 2012 suggesting that billions of dollars could not be accounted for, findings that, despite criticism from some segments of the Nigerian government, were reportedly similar to those of Nigeria's own EITI (NEITI) audits.[19]

Crude Oil Theft in Nigeria and Maritime Piracy in the Gulf of Guinea

Corruption and fraud have long been associated with Nigeria's oil industry. Alleged state-level fraud has been linked to the allocation of state oil revenues, concession licensing, and exploration and extraction permits, but the outright theft of crude, known locally as bunkering, is also a major challenge. Small-scale pilfering and illegal local refining has been, and continues to be, a problem, but large-scale illegal bunkering by sophisticated theft networks is a significant threat with international dimensions. By some estimates, between $3 billion and $8 billion in Nigerian oil is stolen annually.[20] In its 2013 report *Nigeria's Criminal Crude*, the London-based Chatham House estimates that an average of 100,000 barrels per day were stolen in the first quarter of 2013.[21] Niger Delta militants, Nigerian politicians, security officers, and oil industry personnel have been implicated in the theft and illegal trade of Nigerian crude. Challenges in addressing oil theft are compounded by a lack of transparency in the Nigerian oil industry.

Export oil theft networks, to which some of the Niger Delta militant groups are tied, have also been implicated in moving drugs and other illicit materials. Experts suggest that the trade in stolen oil supports the spread of other transnational organized crimes in the Gulf of Guinea, including maritime piracy. Attacks in Nigerian territorial waters account for the overwhelming majority of piracy incidents in the Gulf, and the U.N. Office on Drugs and Crime reports that most of these incidents can be traced back to the Niger Delta and linked to the illegal oil trade.[22]

Despite its status as one of the world's largest crude oil exporters, Nigeria imports an estimated $10 billion in refined fuel annually for domestic consumption, and it suffers periodically from severe fuel and electricity shortages. In an effort to increase its refining capacity and halt oil imports by 2020, the government has granted permits for several new independently owned refineries. In 2010, Nigeria signed an agreement with China worth a reported $23 billion for new refineries, and in 2012 the government signed a memorandum of understanding with U.S.-based Vulcan Petroleum Resources for a $4.5 billion project to build six refineries.

Nigeria's domestic subsidy on gasoline (roughly 70% of which is imported, despite domestic petroleum production) may have limited the attractiveness of refining capacity expansion plans to foreign investors. For years, the government has subsidized the price its citizens pay for fuel, and economists have long deemed the subsidy benefit unsustainable. The subsidy's cost—roughly $8 billion, or 4% of GDP, in 2011—has been steep, comprising almost one-quarter of the government's annual budget. At the recommendation of the International Monetary Fund and others, in late 2011 President Jonathan cut the subsidy, causing the price of gasoline for consumers to double in early 2012 and sparking strong domestic opposition. In the face of mass protests and a nationwide strike, the government backtracked and reinstated a partial subsidy, estimated at 2% of GDP in 2012.[23] Public scrutiny of the program has since increased—in mid-2012 a legislative inquiry revealed that an estimated $7 billion allocated for the subsidy may have

---

[19] NEITI's audits are available at http://www.neiti.org ng.

[20] Christina Katsouris and Aaron Sayne, *Nigeria's Criminal Crude: International Options to Combat the Export of Stolen Oil*, Chatham House, September 2013.

[21] Ibid.

[22] The hijacking of oil tankers and opportunistic robberies are the predominant types of maritime crime in these waters. Kidnapping for ransom is less common, particularly in comparison to acts of piracy off the Horn of Africa. For more information, see UNODC, *Transnational Organized Crime in West Africa: A Threat Assessment*, February 2013.

[23] See, e.g., "Removal of Fuel Subsidies in Nigeria: An Economic Necessity and a Political Dilemma," The Brookings Institution, January 10, 2012.

been misappropriated. The scandal prompted Jonathan to replace several senior executives at the national petroleum company, which was implicated in the scandal. The lawmaker who led the probe, Farouk Lawan, was accused of taking a bribe from one of the companies involved and was replaced in early 2013. Lawan maintained that he took the bribe as evidence.

The government plans to refocus funds saved by decreasing the fuel subsidy on improving health, education, and the nation's power supply. Jonathan has pledged to increase electricity generation tenfold over the next decade, and efforts to privatize power stations and distribution companies are underway, albeit behind schedule, despite objections from the country's trade unions.

In addition to its oil reserves, Nigeria has the ninth-largest natural gas reserves in the world and the largest in Africa, but they have provided comparatively little benefit to the country's economy. Many of Nigeria's oil fields lack the infrastructure to capture and transport natural gas. The government has repeatedly, but unsuccessfully, set deadlines for oil companies to stop "flaring" gas at oil wells (burning unwanted gas during oil drilling), a practice estimated to destroy roughly one-third of annual production and to constitute more than $2 billion in lost revenue annually.[24] In 2011, President Jonathan announced a series of new agreements to develop gas processing facilities as part of a "gas revolution" designed to create new jobs and revenues, and to end flaring. Nigeria is in the process of increasing its liquefied natural gas (LNG) exports, which could surpass revenues derived from oil exports in the next decade.

Financial Sector Reforms

Successive Nigerian administrations have made commitments to economic reform, but their track record is mixed. According to the IMF, reforms initiated under the Obasanjo Administration and continued by his successors, most importantly the policies of maintaining low external debt and budgeting based on a conservative oil price benchmark to create a buffer of foreign reserves, lessened the impact of the 2008-2009 global economic crisis on Nigeria's economy.[25] Oil revenues above the benchmark price had been saved since 2004 in an Excess Crude Account (ECA), although the government drew substantially from the account in 2009-2010 in an effort to stimulate economic recovery. The Jonathan Administration replaced the ECA with a sovereign wealth fund in 2011. The country has made significant gains in the past decade in paying down its external debt, which constituted more than one-third of GDP a decade ago, freeing funding for programs aimed at poverty reduction and reaching the country's Millennium Development Goals.

Like his predecessors, President Jonathan has committed to reforms that aim to attract foreign investment, create jobs, and fuel development, and the U.S. government has been publicly supportive of his economic team.[26] In 2011, he appointed World Bank managing director Ngozi Okonjo-Iweala, who led efforts to reduce Nigeria's debt as Obasanjo's finance minister, to resume her former post. Jonathan has retained Lamido Sanusi as governor of the central bank. Sanusi has led efforts to modernize the country's banking system and tighten banking supervision.[27]

---

[24] U.S. Energy Information Administration, *Country Analysis Brief: Nigeria*, October 16, 2012.

[25] International Monetary Fund, "Staff Report for the Article IV Consultation with Nigeria," July 2012.

[26] Remarks by Assistant Secretary of State Johnnie Carson, "Nigeria, One Year After Elections," Center for Strategic and International Studies, April 9, 2012.

[27] In 2009, Sanusi instituted regulations that require banks to report large cash transactions between accounts if one of the account holders is considered to be "politically exposed." Bank audits ordered by Sanusi that year found 10 banks (continued...)

Social Issues and Security Concerns

Islamic *Sharia* Law

Nigeria is home to one of the world's largest Muslim populations, vying with, and likely outpacing, Egypt as the largest on the continent. The north is predominately Sunni Muslim, and 12 northern states use Islamic *sharia* law to adjudicate criminal and civil matters for Muslims.[28] In some states, the introduction of sharia (from 1999 onward) was a flashpoint between Muslims and Christians. Under the Nigerian constitution, sharia does not apply to non-Muslims in civil and criminal proceedings in these states, but observers note that Islamic mores are often enforced in public without regard for citizens' religion. In some areas, state-funded vigilante groups known as *hisbah* patrol public areas and attempt to enforce sharia-based rulings. Many analysts nonetheless see the interpretation and implementation of Nigerian sharia as moderate in comparison to that of some other Muslim-majority countries.

Religious and Communal Tensions

The U.S. Commission on International Religious Freedom (USCIRF) has recommended since 2009 that Nigeria be classified as a "Country of Particular Concern" for "systematic, ongoing, and egregious violations of religious freedom that lead to particularly severe violations affecting all Nigerians, both Christian and Muslim."[29] It is not designated as such by the Secretary of State. According to USCIRF, as many as 14,000 Nigerians have been killed since 1999 in sectarian violence, and the commissioners argue that the Nigerian government has tolerated the violence, creating a culture of impunity that has emboldened Boko Haram and its sympathizers and been used to exploit Muslim-Christian tensions to destabilize the country. USCIRF has noted ongoing reprisal attacks between Muslim and Christian communities in central Nigeria, the religious nature of the 2011 post-election violence, Boko Haram's attacks against Christians, and rising religiously-charged rhetoric as areas of significant concern. Other experts also point to increasingly well-armed militias, loosely organized along religious lines, in central and northern Nigeria.[30] The State Department, in its annual Religious Freedom report, states that "the government generally respected religious freedom," but criticizes the government's lack of effective efforts to stem communal violence or to investigate and prosecute those responsible.[31]

(...continued)

near collapse due to reckless lending. The government provided $4 billion to rescue the banks, and in late 2010, under pressure from Sanusi, the legislature approved the establishment of the Asset Management Company of Nigeria (AMCON) to buy bad bank loans in exchange for government bonds, in an effort to get the banks lending again. By some estimates it may take a decade for AMCON to divest its toxic assets. AMCON bought non-performing loans from nine rescued banks and margin loans from 12 other domestic banks.

[28] Nigerian law protects freedom of religion and permits states to establish courts based on common law or customary law systems. Non-sharia based common law and customary law courts adjudicate cases involving non-Muslims in these states, and sharia-based criminal law courts are elective for non-Muslims.

[29] U.S. Commission on International Religious Freedom, *Annual Report 2013,* April 2013.

[30] Testimony of Darren Kew, in U.S. Congress, House Subcommittee on Africa, Global Health, and Human Rights, *The Crisis in Christian-Muslim Relations in Nigeria,* 112th Cong., July 10, 2012.

[31] State Department, *July-December 2012 International Religious Freedom Report,* July 2013.

Sectarian violence continues to be a particular problem in and around the central Nigerian city of Jos, the capital of Plateau State, which sits between the predominately Muslim north and Christian south. Tensions among communities in this culturally diverse "Middle Belt" are both religious and ethnic, and they stem from competition over resources—land, education, government jobs—between ethnic groups classified as settlers or as "indigenes" (original inhabitants of the state), with the latter designation conveying certain political and economic benefits. In Jos, the mostly Christian Berom are considered indigenes, and the predominately Muslim Hausa-Fulani, who were traditionally nomadic and pastoralist, are viewed as the settlers. In 2010, the Nigerian government established a special task force composed of both military and police to restore stability in the state; periodic outbreaks of violence have nonetheless continued, and have been exacerbated by attacks on churches attributed to Boko Haram.[32]

Boko Haram and Militant Islam in Nigeria[33]

Boko Haram, a violent Islamist movement in the north, has grown increasingly active and deadly in its attacks against state and civilian targets in Nigeria since 2010, drawing on a narrative of vengeance for state abuses to elicit recruits and sympathizers. By some estimates, more than 3,600 civilians, security forces, and militants have been killed in related violence. The group has focused on a wide range of targets, as discussed below. While attacks attributed to the group have not exclusively, or even primarily, targeted Christians, attacks on churches in several northern and central states may further fuel existing religious tensions. These bombings, which often occur on Sundays or religious holidays to achieve maximum effect, have sparked deadly reprisal attacks by Christians against Muslim civilians. Such attacks may be part of a deliberate effort to foment instability, with the aim of discrediting and delegitimizing the government in these regions by exposing the weakness of its security apparatus and justice mechanisms.

Boko Haram emerged in the early 2000s as a small, radical Sunni Islamic sect that advocated a strict interpretation and implementation of Islamic law for Nigeria. Calling itself *Jama'a Ahl as-Sunna Li-da'wa wa-al Jihad* (JASLWJ; roughly translated from Arabic as "People Committed to the Propagation of the Prophet's Teachings and Jihad"), the group is more popularly known as *Boko Haram* ("Western education is forbidden"), a nickname given by local Hausa-speaking communities to describe its view that Western education and culture have been corrupting influences. It engaged in periodic skirmishes with police during its formative years, but the group's activities were limited in scope and contained within several highly impoverished states in the predominately Muslim northeast.

In July 2009, the government's attempts to stop Boko Haram's attacks on police stations and other government buildings resulted in the death of at least 700 people, a figure that likely includes not only militants, but also security personnel and bystanders. In the course of that violence, the group's leader, Mohammed Yusuf, a charismatic young cleric who had studied in Saudi Arabia, was killed while in police custody.[34] A sizeable number of Yusuf's followers were

---

[32] See, e.g., ICG, *Curbing Violence in Nigeria: The Jos Crisis,* Africa Report No. 196, December 17, 2012.

[33] For more information on Boko Haram, see, e.g., Andrew Walker, *What is Boko Haram?* USIP, May 2012; Jacob Zenn, "Boko Haram's International Connections," *CTC Sentinel,* January 14, 2012; Peter J. Pham, "Boko Haram's Evolving Threat," Africa Security Brief No. 20, April 2012; and Testimony of CRS Specialist Lauren Ploch, in U.S. Congress, House Homeland Security Subcommittee on Counterterrorism and Intelligence, *Boko Haram: Emerging Threat to the U.S. Homeland?,* 112th Cong., November 30, 2011.

[34] "Islamic Death 'Good for Nigeria'," BBC, July 31, 2009.

also killed or arrested. The group appeared to dissipate after the heavy-handed security crackdown, but reemerged a year later, orchestrating a large-scale prison break in September 2010 that freed hundreds, including its own members. Some reports suggest that a small number of Boko Haram militants may have fled to insurgent training camps in the Sahel during this period.

Boko Haram's attacks have since increased substantially in frequency, reach, and lethality, now occurring almost daily in northeast Nigeria (primarily in Borno and Yobe States), and periodically beyond.[35] Attacks attributed to the group have increasingly featured improvised explosive devices (IEDs), car bombs, and suicide attacks. Boko Haram has primarily focused on state and federal targets, such as police stations, but has also targeted civilians in schools, churches, markets, and bars. By U.N. estimates, more than 500 students and 100 teachers have been killed by the militants, who have destroyed some 500 schools in Borno, Yobe, and Adamawa, leaving more than 15,000 students without access to education.[36] Cell phone towers and media houses have also been attacked. The group has assassinated local political leaders and moderate Muslim clerics, and other critics. Bank robberies attributed to the group may contribute to its financing, although authorities warn that criminal groups may also be opportunistically posing as Boko Haram militants.

The bombing of the U.N. building in Abuja on August 24, 2011 marked a major departure from a previously exclusive focus on domestic targets. It was also Boko Haram's first clearly intentional suicide bombing. Boko Haram spokesmen claimed the attack was retribution for the state's heavy-handed security response against its members, referencing U.S. and international "collaboration" with the Nigerian security apparatus. The bombing may indicate an aspiration by some in Boko Haram to move beyond local politics toward an international jihadist agenda, or it may have been an effort to elicit foreign backing for the group's domestic agenda. The Nigerian government linked Boko Haram to the May 2011 kidnapping of two Europeans in northwest Nigeria; the two men were killed in a rescue attempt in early 2012. The group was more recently tied to the kidnapping of a French family in Cameroon, in early 2013; they were later released.

By many accounts, Boko Haram is not a monolithic organization. According to U.S. officials, its core militants may number in the hundreds, but the group also appears to draw support from a broader following of several thousand young men, primarily from the northeast, who have expressed frustration with perceived disparities in the application of laws (including sharia); the lack of development, jobs, and investment in the north; and the heavy-handed response of security forces.[37] Some analysts suggest that Boko Haram is susceptible to fracturing, with a segment of the leadership working to build ties with the international Al Qaeda franchise, while others remain focused exclusively on a domestic agenda. The emergence of a purported splinter faction known as Ansaru in early 2012 led to speculation about divisions among Boko Haram hardliners.[38] Ansaru has been critical of Boko Haram's killing of Nigerian Muslims in its public statements and has primarily focused its attacks on foreigners, primarily through kidnappings.[39]

---

[35] For an account of atrocities attributed to Boko Haram, see, e.g., HRW, *Spiraling Violence: Boko Haram Attacks and Security Force Abuses in Nigeria*, October 11, 2012. For more information on the location and estimated death toll, by week, of Boko Haram attacks, see, e.g., the Council on Foreign Relations' Nigeria Security Tracker at http://www.cfr.org.

[36] U.N. Office for the Coordination of Humanitarian Affairs, "Humanitarian Bulletin Nigeria Issue 7: November 2013," November 12, 2013.

[37] Testimony of Assistant Secretary Linda Thomas-Greenfield, November 13, 2013, op. cit.

[38] Ansaru's full name is *Jama'at Ansar al Muslimin fi Bilad is Sudan* ("Supporters of the Muslims in the Land of the (continued...)

Efforts by various interlocutors to facilitate government negotiations with Boko Haram have been unsuccessful. The state of emergency declared by the Nigerian government in May 2013 for the states of Borno, Yobe, and Adamawa has been extended through May 2014. By U.N. estimates, Boko Haram attacks against soft targets, and associated fighting between militants and security forces, has had a heavy toll on these states during this time.[40] Human rights advocates have urged the Nigerian government not to consider a possible offer of amnesty, similar to that provided to Niger Delta militants (see below) for Boko Haram members involved in the group's most serious abuses. They have also urged the Nigerian security forces to improve efforts to protect civilians as they conduct their offensive against the militants, which has pushed some 40,000 refugees—up from 6,000 refugees in June—across the border into Niger.[41] Some local communities have formed vigilante groups to protect themselves. In Borno State, for example, these groups are now in many cases working with the state government and security forces to rout Boko Haram cells. Press reports suggest that the groups, who collectively call themselves the "Civilian Joint Task Force" or Civilian-JTF, have had some success in improving security in the Borno State capital of Maiduguri, but Boko Haram attacks in rural areas continue.[42]

The Prosecutor of the International Criminal Court (ICC) reported August 2013 that, based on a preliminary investigation, "there is a reasonable basis to believe" that Boko Haram has committed crimes against humanity, namely acts of murder and persecution, resulting in the killing of more than 1,200 Christian and Muslim civilians.[43] The Office of the Prosecutor is now assessing whether Nigerian authorities are conducting "genuine proceedings" against those who may be responsible in order to determine whether a formal investigation by the ICC is warranted.

Boko Haram and Ansaru: An Increasingly Transnational Threat?

While Boko Haram currently appears primarily to pose a threat to local stability, its expansion and purported splintering has amplified concerns that Nigerians may be susceptible to recruitment by Muslim extremist groups aiming to use violence against government or civilian targets elsewhere in the region or abroad. The increasing lethality and sophistication of Boko Haram's attacks has further raised the group's profile among U.S. national security officials, as did reports of Nigerians training in camps in northern Mali in late 2012/early 2013.[44] The rise in kidnappings of Western citizens in northern Nigeria, several of whom have been killed in captivity, is another source of concern as policymakers seek to determine the extent to which Boko Haram, Ansaru, and other violent extremist groups in the region may pose an increasingly transnational threat.[45]

(...continued)

Blacks"). For more information, see, e.g., Jacob Zenn, "Boko Haram's Evolving Tactics and Alliances in Nigeria," *CTC Sentinel,* The Combatting Terrorism Center at West Point, June 25, 2013 and "Cooperation or Competition: Boko Haram and Ansaru After the Mali Intervention, *CTC Sentinel,* March 27, 2013.

[39] See, e.g., "Boko Haram: Splinter Group, Ansaru Emerges," *Vanguard,* February 1, 2012

[40] U.N. OCHA, "Humanitarian Bulletin Nigeria Issue 7: November 2013," November 12, 2013.

[41] "Nigeria Offensive Drives 40,000 Refugees into Niger: U.N.," Reuters, November 13, 2013. According to U.N. estimates, three-quarters of the refugees are officially Niger nationals and the rest are Nigerian.

[42] Adam Nossiter, "Vigilantes Defeat Boko Haram in its Nigerian Base, *New York Times*, October 20, 2013.

[43] The Office of the Prosecutor of the ICC, *Report on Preliminary Examination Activities 2012,* November 2012.

[44] See, e.g., "Timbuktu Training Site Shows Terrorists' Reach," *The Wall Street Journal,* February 1, 2013.

[45] Testimony of National Counterterrorism Center Director Matthew Olsen, Senate Homeland Security and Governmental Affairs Committee, *Threats to the Homeland*, November 14, 2013.

The February 2013 kidnapping of a French family in northern Cameroon is believed to be Boko Haram's first major operation outside Nigeria.

Potential ties with Al Qaeda in the Islamic Maghreb (AQIM), a regional criminal and terrorist network that is designated by the United States as a Foreign Terrorist Organization (FTO), appear to be of particular concern. U.S. Africa Command officials have identified Boko Haram as a "threat to Western interests," referencing indications that the two groups "are likely sharing funds, training, and explosive materials," and suggesting that "there are elements of Boko Haram that aspire to a broader regional level of attacks, to include not just in Africa, but Europe and aspirationally to the United States."[46] The FBI assessed in November 2013 that while "Boko Haram does not currently pose a threat to the Homeland," it does "aspire to attack U.S. or Western interests in the region," and demonstrated its capability to do so with the 2011 U.N. attack.[47] The FBI expressly noted concern with communications, training and weapons links between the group and AQIM, Al Shabaab, and Al Qaeda in the Arabian Peninsula (AQAP).

Deliberations within the U.S. government over whether to designate Boko Haram as an FTO (see "Congressional Engagement") concluded in November 2013, when the State Department designated both Boko Haram and Ansaru as FTOs under Section 219 of the Immigration and Nationality Act, as amended, and as Specially Designated Global Terrorists (SDGTs) under Executive Order 13224.[48] The FTO designations aim to assist U.S. and other law enforcement agencies in efforts to investigate and prosecute suspects associated with the group, and have been described by U.S. officials as important step in supporting the Nigerian government's effort to address the threat.[49] The State Department had previously designated three individuals linked to Boko Haram as SGDTs in June 2012, including Boko Haram leader Abubakar Shekau, and in 2013 issued a $7 million reward for information on the location of Shekau through its Rewards for Justice program.[50] The Nigerian government also formally designated Boko Haram and Ansaru as terrorist groups in 2013. The British government had named Ansaru as a "Proscribed Terrorist Organization" in 2012, describing it as broadly aligned with Al Qaeda, and designated Boko Haram as such in July, 2013. These groups are not currently included in the U.N. Al Qaeda sanctions list, to which two Mali-based groups affiliated with AQIM were recently added.

---

[46] Remarks by Gen. Carter Ham, Africa Center for Strategic Studies Senior Leaders Seminar, June 25, 2012; and Testimony of Gen. Ham, Senate Armed Services Committee, *Proposed FY2013 Defense Authorization as it Relates to the U.S. European and Africa Commands,* March 1, 2012 and House Armed Services Committee, *Proposed Fiscal 2014 Defense Authorization as it Relates to the U.S. European and Africa Commands,* March 15, 2013.

[47] Testimony of FBI Director James Comey, Senate Homeland Security and Governmental Affairs Committee, *Threats to the Homeland,* November 14, 2013.

[48] The FTO designation triggers the freezing of any assets a group might have in U.S. financial institutions, bans FTO members' travel to the United States, and criminalizes transactions (including material support) with the organization or its members. It is unclear, given the current lack of public information available on Boko Haram's possible ties abroad, if these measures would have any impact on the group. While FTO status might serve to prioritize greater U.S. security and intelligence resources toward the group, this is not a legal requirement of the designation.

[49] State Department, Daily News Briefing, November 13, 2013.

[50] Shekau, along with Khalid al-Barnawi and Abubakar Adam Kambar, both of whom have ties to Boko Haram and close links to AQIM, according to the State Department, have been designated as SDGTs.

Conflict in the Niger Delta

Nigeria's oil wealth has long been a source of political tension, protest, and criminality in the Niger Delta region, where most of the country's oil is produced.[51] Compared to Nigeria's national average, the region's social indicators are low, and unemployment is high. Millions of barrels of oil are believed to have been spilled in the region since oil production began, causing major damage to the fragile riverine ecosystem, and ultimately to the livelihoods of many of the Delta's 30 million inhabitants.[52] Gas flares have further plagued the Delta with acid rain and air pollution, limiting locals' access to clean water and destroying fishing stocks that the majority of Delta inhabitants depended on to make a living.

Conflict in the Niger Delta has been marked by the vandalism of oil infrastructures; massive, systemic production theft locally known as "oil bunkering," often abetted by state officials; protests over widespread environmental damage caused by oil operations; kidnapping for ransom; and public insecurity and communal violence. The demands of the region's various militant groups have varied, but often include calls for greater autonomy for the region and a larger share of oil revenues. Militant groups like the Movement for the Emancipation of the Niger Delta (MEND) have used the kidnapping of oil workers and attacks on oil facilities to bring international attention to the Delta's plight. These attacks have periodically cut Nigeria's oil production by as much as 25%, and have been blamed for spikes in the world price of oil. Nigeria's deep-water production has also proven vulnerable to militant attacks, and the threat of sea piracy is high. By some estimates, up to 10% of Nigeria's oil has been stolen annually, and local politicians have reportedly financed their campaigns through such criminal activities.[53]

Successive Nigerian governments have pledged to engage the Delta's disaffected communities, but few of their efforts met with success until 2009, when President Yar'Adua extended an offer of amnesty to Delta militants. Under the offer, those who surrendered their weapons, renounced violence, and accepted rehabilitation were granted a presidential pardon, along with cash and job training. According to Nigerian government estimates, more than 26,000 have benefitted from the program, which is costing the government roughly $400 million a year, though it is unclear whether all were directly involved in militancy. While the activities of criminal gangs have continued, the UN Office on Drugs and Crime suggests in its 2013 report on transnational criminal organizations in West Africa that the number of recorded attacks on the oil industry—including bombings, kidnappings, hijackings, and acts of piracy—has declined remarkably" since the amnesty effort began, and contends that "the link between political activism and oil theft has grown increasingly tenuous since 2011."[54]

---

[51] In the early 1990s, activists from the Ogoni ethnic group drew international attention to the extensive environmental damage done by oil extraction in the Niger Delta. Author and activist Ken Saro-Wiwa, president of the Movement for the Survival of the Ogoni People (MOSOP), and 14 others were accused in 1994 of involvement in the murder of several prominent Ogoni politicians. They pled not guilty, but Saro-Wiwa and eight others were convicted and sentenced to death. Their executions sparked international outrage against the regime of dictator Sani Abacha, and the United States recalled its ambassador in response.

[52] UNEP, *Environmental Assessment of Ogoniland*, 2011; UNDP, *Niger Delta Human Development Report*, 2006; Amnesty International, *Petroleum, Pollution, and Poverty in the Niger Delta*, June 2009; and Paul Francis, Deirdre Lapin, and Paula Rossiasco, *Securing Development and Peace in the Niger Delta*, Woodrow Wilson Center, 2011.

[53] HRW, *Criminal Politics: Violence, "Godfathers" and Corruption in Nigeria*, Vol. 19, No. 16(A), October 2007.

[54] MEND, for example, had previously admitted to being involved in such activities, which it justified as a reappropriation of wealth and form of protest. UNODC, *Transnational Organized Crime in West Africa*, op.cit.

President Jonathan has continued to allocate significant financing for "post-amnesty" interventions and development projects in the Delta, targeting transport, education, and health infrastructure. Concerns remain regarding the government's ability to spend the funds effectively in a region where corruption is, at all levels, endemic, and some Nigerian politicians from other regions have criticized the cost of the program.[55] Some of the oil-producing states have reported revenues of over $2 billion per year but have dismal records of development or service delivery.[56] The federal government's commitment and ability to deliver on promised infrastructure improvements and job creation will be critical to addressing regional grievances. Observers caution that unless the root causes of conflict are addressed, the Delta will remain volatile.

Abuses by Security Forces

Nigerian security forces, particularly the police, but also the military, have been accused of serious human rights abuses, and both activists and U.S. officials suggest that the government has done little to address issues of impunity and corruption within the police force.[57] The U.N. Special Rapporteur on Torture has reported that "torture is an intrinsic part of how law enforcement services operate within the country," and called on the Nigerian government to criminalize the practice.[58] The State Department's 2012 human rights report documents allegations by multiple sources of "arbitrary or unlawful killings" by security forces, including "summary executions ... torture, rape and other cruel, inhuman, or degrading treatment of prisoners, detainees, and criminal suspects," and a variety of other offenses, such as the use of "excessive force to stem civil unrest and interethnic violence." The prison system has also drawn criticism; human rights groups report that many of the country's inmates are incarcerated for years without being convicted of a crime. The security crackdown on Boko Haram in the northeast has recently drawn particular attention—Amnesty International reports that more than 950 people may have died in military detention centers in the first six months of 2013 alone, many of them at select sites in Borno and Yobe States, and suggests that the government continues to restrict human rights investigators from accessing these facilities.[59]

In the past decade, the Nigerian government has deployed Joint Task Forces (JTFs), special combined military and police units, to respond to specific conflicts that the government classifies as national emergencies. The first JTF was established in the Niger Delta. In 2009, it launched an offensive against Delta militants during which thousands of civilians were reportedly displaced, according to Amnesty International.[60] Armed conflict between security forces and Delta militia has decreased with the amnesty program, although periodic attacks and skirmishes continue. JTFs have also been deployed to stem the communal violence in Jos and to address the Boko Haram threat in the northeast.

---

[55] Xan Rice, "Nigerian Rebels Swap Weapons for Welding," *Washington Post*, July 5, 2012.

[56] Francis, Lapin, and Rossiasco, *Securing Development and Peace in the Niger Delta*, op. cit.

[57] Recent reports on abuses include HRW, *Arbitrary Killings by Security Forces* and *Spiraling Violence*, op. cit.; Amnesty International, *Killing at Will: Extrajudicial Executions and Other Unlawful Killings by the Police in Nigeria* and *Nigeria: Trapped in the Cycle of Violence*; and *Criminal Force: Torture, Abuse, and Extrajudicial Killings by the Nigerian Police Force*, by the Open Society Justice Initiative and the Network of Police Reform in Nigeria.

[58] United Nations Press Release, "Special Rapporteur on Torture Concludes Visit to Nigeria," March 12, 2007.

[59] Amnesty International "Nigeria: Authorities Must Allow Human Rights Commission to Audit Military Detention Centres," November 12, 2013, and "Nigeria: Authorities Must Investigate Deaths of Boko Haram Suspects in Military Custody," October 15, 2013.

[60] Amnesty International, "Hundreds Feared Dead and Thousands Trapped in Niger Delta Fighting," May 22, 2009.

Forces deployed under the JTF to counter Islamist militants in the northeast—JTF-Operation Restore Order—have been implicated in extrajudicial killings of suspected militants and in civilian deaths. In April 2013, for example, more than 180 people were killed in fighting between security forces and suspected Boko Haram militants in the village of Baga, according to the Red Cross and local officials; among the dead were reportedly innocent bystanders, including children.[61] Nigerian security forces disputed the number of casualties. Satellite imagery suggests that more than 2,000 homes may have been burned.[62] U.N. reporting suggests than almost 1,200 civilians, insurgents, and military personnel have been killed in the first six months of the state of emergency (declared in May 2013)[63]

Nigerian officials have acknowledged some abuses by security forces, but few security personnel have been prosecuted.[64] In its most recent human rights report, the State Department suggests there have been no new developments in the case against police officers accused of executing Boko Haram founder Muhammed Yusuf; four of the five officers were granted bail in 2011.

HIV/AIDS, Education, and Population Growth

Nigeria's HIV/AIDS prevalence rate of 3.6% is relatively low in comparison to Southern African nations with adult seropositivity rates of 10 to 25%. However, the West African nation comprises nearly one-tenth of the world's HIV/AIDS infected persons with more than 3 million people infected, the largest HIV-positive population in the world after South Africa. Nigeria's population is expected to double by the year 2025, which is likely to multiply the spread of HIV. In addition to the devastation HIV/AIDS continues to cause among Nigeria's adult population, over 40% of the current population is under the age of 15. With almost a third of primary-school-aged children not enrolled in school and a large number of HIV/AIDS-infected adults, Nigeria faces serious challenges and significant obstacles in the education and health care sectors.

International Relations

Nigeria has been an important player in regional and international affairs since the 1990s, although domestic challenges may distract the Jonathan Administration from playing a more robust regional role in the near term. The government has mediated political disputes in Togo, Mauritania, Liberia, Sudan, and Cote d'Ivoire, and has been engaged in regional efforts to resolve the political and security crisis in Mali. Nigeria was critical of the international community for "contradictions" in its reaction to the recent crises in Cote d'Ivoire and Libya, questioning the comparatively robust Western response to protect civilians in Libya.[65] Nigerian troops played a central role in regional peacekeeping operations in Sierra Leone and Liberia, and have also participated in the peacekeeping mission in Mali. Nigerian police, military observers, and experts are deployed in U.N. missions in Cote d'Ivoire, the Democratic Republic of Congo, Haiti, Timor-Leste, Sudan, South Sudan, and Western Sahara, and they play a limited role in the U.N.-supported AU mission in Somalia.

---

[61] See, e.g., "Scores Killed in Nigeria Violence," Al Jazeera, April 23, 2013.

[62] Human Rights Watch, "Nigeria: Massive Destruction, Deaths from Military Raid," May 1, 2013.

[63] U.N. OCHA, "Humanitarian Bulletin Nigeria Issue 7: November 2013," November 12, 2013.

[64] "Nigeria Condemns Police 'Killing'," BBC, March 5, 2010.

[65] "Nigeria Lashes at World's Focus on Libya While I. Coast Burns," AFP, March 22, 2011.

The country is a member of the Organization of the Petroleum Exporting Countries (OPEC) and the Economic Community of West African States (ECOWAS). The United States is the top destination for Nigerian exports, followed by India, Brazil, Spain, and France. China is the lead source for Nigerian imports, followed by the United States, the Netherlands, South Korea, and the United Kingdom.[66] Nigeria has become a major destination for Chinese investment in Africa.

Issues for Congress

Administration Policy on Nigeria

After a period of strained relations in the 1990s, when Nigeria had a military dictatorship, U.S.-Nigeria relations steadily improved under President Obasanjo, and they have remained robust under Presidents Yar'Adua and Jonathan. Diplomatic engagement is sometimes tempered, however, by Nigerian perceptions of U.S. intrusion in regional or domestic affairs, and by U.S. concern with human rights, governance, and corruption issues. President Obama's former Assistant Secretary of State for African Affairs Johnnie Carson often referred to Nigeria as "probably the most strategically important country in Sub-Saharan Africa," and his successor, Linda Thomas-Greenfield, has described the country as "one of our most important partners in Africa."[67] That partnership may take on additional importance when Nigeria joins the U.N. Security Council as one of its non-permanent members in January 2014, for a two-year term. In addition the strategic role their country plays in the region and in global forums, Nigerians comprise the largest African diaspora group in the United States.

The United States has been supportive of Nigerian reform initiatives, including anti-corruption efforts, economic and electoral reforms, energy sector privatization, and programs to promote peace and development in the Niger Delta. In 2010, the Obama and Jonathan Administrations established the U.S.-Nigeria Binational Commission (BNC), a strategic dialogue to address issues of mutual concern; its working groups meet regularly. The State Department maintains "American Corners," located in libraries throughout the country, to share information on the culture and values of the United States with Nigerians, and it has proposed to eventually expand its presence, perhaps through a new consulate in the northern city of Kano to increase outreach in the north, when security conditions allow. The State Department maintains a travel warning for U.S. citizens regarding travel to Nigeria, noting the risks of armed attacks in the Niger Delta and the northeast, and the threat of piracy in the Gulf of Guinea, and currently restricts U.S. officials from all but essential travel to all northern states.[68]

U.S.-Nigeria Trade and Maritime Security Issues

Nigeria is an important trading partner for the United States and is the second largest beneficiary of U.S. investment on the continent. Given Nigeria's ranking as one of Africa's largest consumer markets and its affinity for U.S. products and American culture, opportunities for increasing U.S.

---

[66] CIA, "Nigeria," *The World Factbook 2013.*

[67] State Department, "Remarks by Ambassador Carson on Secretary Clinton's Africa Trip," July 30, 2009; Remarks by Assistant Secretary Carson, "Promise and Peril in Nigeria: Implications for U.S. Engagement," at CSIS, April 9, 2012; Testimony of Linda Thomas-Greenfield, November 13, 2013, op. cit.

[68] See http://travel.state.gov for the latest warning.

exports to the country, and the broader West Africa region, are considerable, although U.S. imports from Nigeria far outweigh exports.[69] The Obama Administration aims to double U.S. exports to Nigeria by 2015 through the President's National Export Initiative. The country is eligible for trade benefits under the African Growth and Opportunity Act (AGOA). AGOA-eligible exports, nearly all of which are petroleum products, have accounted for over 90% of exports to the United States.

Gulf of Guinea crude is prized on the world market for its low sulphur content, and Nigeria's proximity to the United States relative to that of Middle East countries has made its oil particularly attractive to U.S. interests. The country has regularly ranked among the United States' largest sources of imported oil. U.S. imports, which accounted for over 40% of Nigeria's total crude oil exports until 2012, have made the United States Nigeria's largest trading partner, although U.S. purchases of Nigerian sweet crude dropped in 2012 and 2013 as domestic U.S. crude supply increased. U.S. energy companies may face increasing competition for rights to the country's energy resources; China, for example, has offered Nigeria favorable loans for infrastructure projects in exchange for oil exploration rights. The U.S. Export-Import (Ex-Im) Bank signed an agreement in 2011 with the Nigerian government that aims to secure up to $1.5 billion in U.S. exports of goods and services to support power generation reforms. A U.S. trade delegation composed of government officials, Ex-Im Bank executives, and energy companies traveled to Nigeria in 2012 to discuss the participation of American companies in the development of Nigeria's energy infrastructure. The Administration has identified Nigeria as one of six initial partner countries for its Power Africa initiative, which aims to double access to power in sub-Saharan Africa.[70]

Given Nigeria's strategic position along the coast of the Gulf of Guinea, the United States has coordinated with Nigeria through various regional forums and maritime security initiatives.[71] Nigeria's waters have been named among the most dangerous in the world; the country ranked first in global pirate attacks until it was overtaken by Somalia in 2008, according to the International Maritime Bureau; it appears to have again overtaken Somalia in the past year. Nigeria is also considered a growing transshipment hub for narcotics trafficking, and several Nigerian criminal organizations have been implicated in the trade. The U.S. Navy has increased its operations in the Gulf of Guinea in recent years and in 2007 launched the African Partnership Station (APS).[72] APS deployments have included port visits to Nigeria and joint exercises between U.S., Nigerian, European, and other regional navies.

---

[69] U.S. Commercial Service, *Doing Business in Nigeria: 2012 Country Commercial Guide for U.S. Companies*.

[70] See The White House, *Fact Sheet: Power Africa*, June 30, 2013.

[71] For further information on maritime and port security issues in the region, see, e.g., the Atlantic Council, *Advancing U.S., African, and Global Interests: Security and Stability in the West African Maritime Domain*, November 30, 2010; and CDR Michael Baker, "Toward an African Maritime Economy," *Naval War College Review*, Vol. 64, Spring 2011; and Chatham House, *Maritime Security in the Gulf of Guinea*, March 2013.

[72] Under APS, U.S. and partner naval ships deploy to the region for several months to serve as a continuing sea base of operations and a "floating schoolhouse" to provide assistance and training to the Gulf nations. Training focuses on maritime domain awareness and law enforcement, port facilities management and security, seamanship/navigation, search and rescue, leadership, logistics, civil engineering, humanitarian assistance and disaster response.

Nigeria's Role in Regional Stability and Counterterrorism Efforts

Nigeria has played a significant role in peace and stability operations across Africa, and the United States continues to provide the country with security assistance focused on enhancing its peacekeeping capabilities. Bilateral counterterrorism cooperation has reportedly improved in the aftermath of the December 2009 airliner bombing attempt and the rise in the Boko Haram threat, although there are still limits to that cooperation.[73] The Nigerian government has coordinated with the Department of Homeland Security, the Federal Aviation Administration, and the International Civil Aviation Organization to strengthen its security systems, and the country now uses full body scanners in its international airports. Nigeria is a participant in the State Department's Trans Sahara Counterterrorism Partnership (TSCTP), a U.S. interagency effort that aims to increase regional counter-terrorism capabilities and coordination. Its role in that program has been to date, minor in comparison to Sahel countries. In view of the reported expansion of Boko Haram operations, including into Cameroon, U.S. officials may explore additional programs to improve counterterrorism coordination between Nigeria and its neighbors, although tensions in some of those relationships may hamper greater cooperation.

Many U.S. officials, while stressing the importance of the U.S-Nigeria relationship and the gravity of security threats in, and potentially emanating from, the country, remain concerned about reported abuses by Nigerian security services, and about the government's limited efforts to address perceived impunity for such abuses. Conversely, some Nigerian officials reportedly remain sensitive to perceived U.S. interference in internal affairs and dismissive of certain training offers. These factors appear to have constrained U.S.-Nigerian security cooperation, despite shared concerns over terrorism and other regional security threats.[74]

The Obama Administration has nevertheless committed, through the BNC dialogue, to support Nigerian efforts to increase public confidence in the military and police to respond more effectively to the threat posed by extremists. In addition to USAID programs to counter radicalization in Nigeria, the State Department and DOD continue to deliberate on how best to support a shift by Nigeria to "an integrated civilian-security-focused strategy to counter Boko Haram and Ansaru in a manner that adheres to the rule of law and ensures accountability."[75]

Reported links between Boko Haram and extremists in Mali, particularly AQIM, may have contributed to Nigerian motivations for initially engaging in regional peacekeeping operations in Mali in 2013. The United States has provided logistical support for peacekeepers in Mali, who are now under a U.N. mandate, although U.S. assistance to the Nigerian forces initially deployed was constrained by the human rights concerns noted above.[76] Nigeria announced its decision to withdraw from the Mali mission, now known as MINUSMA, in July 2013, based on its stated need to prioritize the security situation in northern Nigeria. Some observers questioned whether the decision might be linked to the U.N.'s decision to appoint a Rwandan to lead the mission,

---

[73] On December 25, 2009, Umar Farouk Abdulmutallab, the son of a respected Nigerian banker and former government minister, attempted to detonate an explosive device onboard an American airliner bound from Amsterdam to Detroit. He reportedly became radicalized while living abroad. Al Qaeda in the Arabian Peninsula (AQAP) claims to have sponsored the effort.

[74] See, e.g., On Terror's New Front Line, Mistrust Blunts U.S. Strategy," *The Wall Street Journal*, February 26, 2013.

[75] Testimony of Assistant Secretary of State Linda Thomas-Greenfield, November 13, 2013, op. cit.

[76] The initial Nigerian forces deployed to Mali were reportedly part of a unit linked by human rights groups to serious alleged abuses against civilians and detainees in northeast Nigeria. See HRW, *Spiraling Violence*, op. cit.

---

thereby replacing the Nigerian general who had led the preceding AU operation. MINUSMA continues to face a critical troop shortage, a problem further exacerbated by the Nigerian pullout.

U.S. Assistance to Nigeria

Nigeria routinely ranks among the top recipients of U.S. bilateral foreign assistance in Africa. The United States is Nigeria's largest bilateral donor, providing almost $700 million annually in recent years (see **Table 1**).[77] The State Department's FY2014 foreign aid request includes more than $690 million for Nigeria. Strengthening democratic governance, improving agricultural productivity and access to education and health services, promoting new jobs and increased supplies of clean energy, and professionalizing and reforming the security services have been the main areas of focus in recent years. The State Department has stressed efforts to incorporate conflict prevention and mitigation throughout its foreign assistance programming in Nigeria in its FY2014 budget request. Nigeria is a focus country under the President's Emergency Plan for AIDS Relief (PEPFAR) and the President's Malaria Initiative (PMI), and Nigerian farmers benefit from agriculture programs under the Feed the Future (FTF) initiative that focus on building partnerships with the private sector to expand exports and generate employment. In the Niger Delta, for example, USAID has paired with Chevron on a four-year, $50 million program (of which USAID is contributing half) to improve agricultural development as well as civil society and governance capacity. Interventions to encourage private sector participation in trade and energy, in partnership with the Nigerian government, are also key components of the Obama Administration's economic growth initiatives in Nigeria.

The State Department has focused security assistance requests in recent years on military professionalization, peacekeeping support and training, and border and maritime security. U.S. officials reportedly stress the importance of civilian oversight of the military, and respect for human rights and the rule of law, in their engagements with Nigerian military officials.[78] In addition to peacekeeping support provided through the State Department's African Contingency Operations Training and Assistance (ACOTA) program, Nigeria also benefits from security cooperation activities with the California National Guard through the National Guard State Partnership Program. Nigeria also receives counterterrorism, anticorruption, and maritime security assistance through the State Department's West Africa Regional Security Initiative (WARSI). U.S. counterterrorism assistance to Nigeria includes programs coordinated through TSCTP and other State Department initiatives, including Anti-Terrorism Assistance (ATA), as well as through Department of Defense funds. Nigeria was the first sub-Saharan African country to be named by the Secretary of State to be eligible for counterterrorism and border security assistance under the new Global Security Contingency Fund (GSCF), to be jointly funded by the Departments of State and Defense. Some U.S. assistance for Nigerian military and police units has been restricted based human rights concerns. In this context, U.S. counterterrorism-related training and assistance for Nigerian troops has been constrained, to date, by the Nigerian military's practice of rotating its forces for short-term missions in the northeast, where some individuals and units have been implicated in serious abuses against civilians and detainees.

---

[77] For further information on current U.S. assistance programs, see, e.g., Testimony of USAID Assistant Administrator for Africa Earl Gast, in U.S. Congress, House Subcommittee on Africa, Global Health, and Human Rights, *U.S. Policy Toward Nigeria: West Africa's Troubled Titan,* July 10, 2012.

[78] Remarks by Ambassador Terence P. McCulley at the National Defense College in Abuja, April 26, 2012.

Table 1. State Department and USAID Assistance to Nigeria

($ in thousands)	FY2012 Actual	FY2013 Estimate	FY2014 Request
Development Assistance	50,291	76,920	80,440
Foreign Military Financing	1,000	949	1,000
Global Health Programs – State	461,227	455,746	441,225
Global Health Programs – USAID	133,500	165,451	169,200
International Military Education and Training	926	712	730
Nonproliferation, Antiterrorism, Demining and Related Programs	0	0	100
TOTAL	646,944	699,778	692,695

Source: State Department FY2014 Congressional Budget Justification for Foreign Operations and updated FY2013 figures provided by the State Department in October 2013. Totals do not include emergency humanitarian assistance or certain types of security and development assistance provided through regional programs, including for counterterrorism and peacekeeping purposes.

Congressional Engagement

Terrorism-related concerns have dominated congressional action on Nigeria in the 113th Congress, although some Members also continue to monitor human rights and humanitarian issues, developments in the Niger Delta, and Nigeria's energy sector in the context of world oil supplies. The Africa subcommittees in both houses have held hearings on Nigeria to consider U.S. policy on governance, security and trade issues in the country. The House Homeland Security Committee, whose Subcommittee on Counterterrorism and Intelligence held Congress's first hearing to examine Boko Haram in late 2011, continues to raise concerns about the dearth of information available on the group and the potential to underestimate Boko Haram's potential threat to U.S. interests.[79] Prior to the State Department's decision in November 2013 to designate the group as an FTO, several Members of Congress introduced legislation, including H.R. 3209 and S. 198, to press the Obama Administration on the FTO issue. The FY2013 National Defense Authorization Act (NDAA; P.L. 112-239) directed the Director of National Intelligence (DNI) to provide an assessment of the Boko Haram threat to Congress. In April 2013 testimony before the Senate Armed Services Committee on emerging threats, Assistant Secretary of Defense for International Security Affairs Derek Chollet listed Boko Haram, among other groups, as part of a "metastasizing" threat of locally-focused extremist groups that "can be expected to turn to international targeting if left unopposed." Congressional attention to these and other issues is expected to continue in 2014.

---

[79] See House Homeland Security Subcommittee on Counterterrorism and Intelligence, *Boko Haram: Emerging Threat to the U.S. Homeland*, committee print, 112th Cong., November 30, 2011 and House Homeland Security Committee, *Boko Haram: Growing Threat to the U.S. Homeland*, committee print, 113th Cong., September 13, 2013.

Deliberations Related to the Designation of Boko Haram as an FTO

Some Members of Congress had pressed for the designation of Boko Haram as an FTO for several years before the State Department chose to do so in November 2013.[80] Some Nigeria experts who opposed the designation cautioned that the Nigerian government's response to Boko Haram was heavy-handed and that a designation might actually fuel radical recruitment. Some argued that an FTO designation might be seen, by both the Nigerian government and the northern population, as an endorsement by the United States of "excessive use of force at a time when the rule of law in Nigeria hangs in the balance."[81] Others suggested that Boko Haram's shift toward Christian targets was tactical, and cautioned that U.S. policymakers avoid taking positions that might fuel perceptions that the United States has "taken sides" among Christians and Muslims.[82] Additional arguments against an FTO designation focused on concerns that the label would enhance Boko Haram's status among international extremist groups and internationalize its standing, potentially serving as a fundraising and recruitment tool. State Department officials have noted that, in the course of the extensive interagency process involved in making the determination, they sought to "deepen [their] understanding of the organization," suggesting that Boko Haram's "decentralized and factionalized" nature, with its "loose command-and-control structure," complicated the process.[83]

State Department officials have acknowledged human rights concerns and called on the Nigerian government to "change their strategy with regard to Boko Haram from a primarily military response to one that also addresses the grievances felt by many in northern Nigeria."[84] When Secretary of State John Kerry visited the region in in mid-2013, he raised the issue with Nigerian officials, stating, "one person's atrocity does not excuse another's."[85] The State Department's senior Africa official has urged the Nigerian government to take a more "holistic" approach, suggesting that regional and socioeconomic disparities have contributed to Boko Haram recruitment, and that the government's response should incorporate not only efforts to degrade the group's capacity, but also to provide justice and ensure accountability "in instances where government officials and security forces violate those [human] rights," in part to "diminish Boko Haram's appeal and legitimacy" among would-be recruits.[86]

Author Contact Information

Lauren Ploch
Specialist in African Affairs
lploch@crs.loc.gov, 7-7640

---

[80] The FTO designation derives from authorities granted to the Secretary of State in the Immigration and Nationality Act, as amended. The designation triggers the freezing of any assets in U.S. financial institutions, bans FTO members' travel to the United States, and criminalizes transactions (including material support) with the organization or its members. It is unclear, given the current lack of public information available on Boko Haram's possible ties abroad, if these measures would have any impact on the group. FTO status might serve to prioritize greater U.S. security and intelligence resources toward the group, although this is not a legal requirement of the designation.

[81] Letter to Secretary Clinton by 21 American academics with Nigeria expertise on May 2012.

[82] D. Kew, op. cit.

[83] State Department, Daily News Briefing, November 13, 2013.

[84] Testimony of State Department Coordinator for Counterterrorism Daniel Benjamin, in U.S. Congress, House Foreign Affairs Committee, *LRA, Boko Haram, al-Shabaab, AQIM and Other Sources of Instability in Africa*, April 25, 2012.

[85] "Kerry Criticizes Nigeria on Human Rights," CNN, May 25, 2013.

[86] Testimony of Assistant Secretary of State Linda Thomas-Greenfield, November 13, 2013, op. cit.